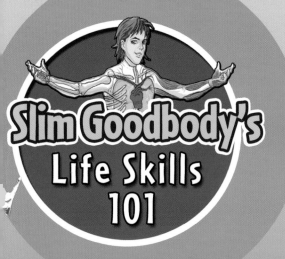

Slim Goodbody's Life Skills 101

CAN WE GET ALONG?

Dealing with Differences

CRABTREE
Publishing Company
www.crabtreebooks.com

Crabtree Publishing Company
www.crabtreebooks.com

Series Development, Writing, and Packaging:
John Burstein, Slim Goodbody Corp.

Editors:
Reagan Miller, Valerie Weber, and Mark Sachner,
  Water Buffalo Books

Editorial director:
Kathy Middleton

Production coordinator:
Kenneth Wright

Prepress technicians:
Margaret Amy Salter, Kenneth Wright

Designer: Tammy West, Westgraphix LLC.

Photos: Chris Pinchback, Pinchback Photography

"Slim Goodbody" and Pinchback photos, copyright,
© Slim Goodbody

"Slim Goodbody" and "Slim Goodbody's Life
Skills 101" are registered trademarks of the Slim
Goodbody Corp.

Photo credits:
iStockPhotos: p. 4 (top), 6 (bottom left), 11 (top 2),
  13 (right), 17 (right), 18 (top right), 22 (all), 29
Shutterstock: p. 4 (bottom), 6 (bottom right), 7 (all),
  9, 10 (top,), 11 (bottom 3), 12 (bottom), 13 (left),
  14 (all), 15, 16 (middle, bottom), 17 (left), 18
  (middle, bottom left, right), 19, 23 (all), 25, 26,
  27 (bottom)
© Slim Goodbody: p. 1, 5, 6 (top), 8 (all), 12 (top),
  16 (top), 18 (top), 20 (all), 21 (all), 24, 27 (top), 28
Wikipedia: Agência Brasil/Fabio Pozzebom: p. 10
  (middle); "Foundation of Holy Defence Values,
  Archives and Publications"/www.sajed.ir:
  p. 10 (bottom)

Acknowledgements:
The author would like to thank the following
children for all their help in this project: Stephanie
Bartlett , Sarah Booth, Christine Burstein, Lucas
Burstein, Olivia Davis, Eleni Fernald, Kylie Fong,
Tristan Fong, Colby Hill, Carrie Laurita, Ginny
Laurita, Henry Laurita, Louis Laurita, Nathan Levig,
Havana Lyman, Renaissance Lyman, Andrew
McBride, Lulu McClure, Yanmei McElhaney,
Amanda Mirabile, Esme Power, Emily Pratt,
Andrew Smith, Dylan Smith, Mary Wells

Library and Archives Canada Cataloguing in Publication

Burstein, John
    Can we get along? : dealing with differences / John Burstein.

(Slim Goodbody's life skills 101)
Includes index.
ISBN 978-0-7787-4788-8 (bound).--ISBN 978-0-7787-4804-5 (pbk.)

    1. Toleration--Juvenile literature. I. Title. II. Title: Dealing
with differences. III. Series: Burstein, John. Slim Goodbody's
life skills 101

HM1271.B87 2010   j179'.9   C2009-903735-1

Library of Congress Cataloging-in-Publication Data

Burstein, John.
    Can we get along? : dealing with differences / John Burstein.
       p. cm. -- (Slim goodbody's life skills 101)
    Includes index.
    ISBN 978-0-7787-4804-5 (pbk. : alk. paper) -- ISBN 978-0-7787-4788-8 (reinforced
library binding : alk. paper)
    1. Toleration. I. Title. II. Series.

    HM1271.B87 2010
    179'.9--dc22

                                              2009023634

Crabtree Publishing Company

www.crabtreebooks.com   1-800-387-7650

Published in Canada
Crabtree Publishing
616 Welland Ave.
St. Catharines, Ontario
L2M 5V6

Published in the United States
Crabtree Publishing
PMB16A
350 Fifth Ave., Suite 3308
New York, NY 10118

Published in the United Kingdom
Crabtree Publishing
White Cross Mills
High Town, Lancaster
LA1 4XS

Published in Australia
Crabtree Publishing
386 Mt. Alexander Rd.
Ascot Vale (Melbourne)
VIC 3032

CONTENTS

Words in bold are defined
in the glossary on page 30.

A PLAYGROUND FIGHT

Kaitlin was furious. That dorky shrimp, Kalil Mustara, was making fun of her on the playground.

"How dare he call me names," she thought.

"Hey, Frizzy Top!" Kalil yelled again. "What did you do, stick your finger in the light socket?"

Kaitlin's hair was the curliest in the class. But no one had the right to call her Frizzy Top!

She'd make Kalil sorry for insulting her. "I'm surprised you can even see my hair from way down there, Shorty." She heard some kids start to laugh.

Kalil was the smallest kid in the class. He hated it when people made fun of his height.

"Take that back, or I'll make you regret it," Kalil shouted. He shook his fist.

"I didn't think people from your country knew how to fight," said Kaitlin.

"This is my country!" snapped Kalil.

"Then why do you talk with such a funny accent?" Kaitlin said with a sneer.

A crowd of kids circled the two of them. They chanted, "Fight, fight, fight, fight!"

Kaitlin felt scared. So did Kalil. Each of them was wondering, "How can I get out of this?"

Hi. My name is Slim Goodbody.

I think one of the saddest things in the world is to see people being hurtful to one another. Often, people treat others badly just because they seem strange or different. I wrote this book to help you see through these differences to the important things that all people have in common.

Working Together

We will explore how to get along better with one another. I will ask you to do some serious thinking about how you deal with people who seem different. Examining your beliefs takes work, but the effort is worth it. If we all work together, we can build a more peaceful and caring world.

A WORLD OF DIFFERENCE

There are more than six-and-a-half-billion people living on Earth. Every single one of these people is different than you and different from everyone else. Each person is a unique, special, one-of-a-kind human being. These differences make the world a truly wonderful place.

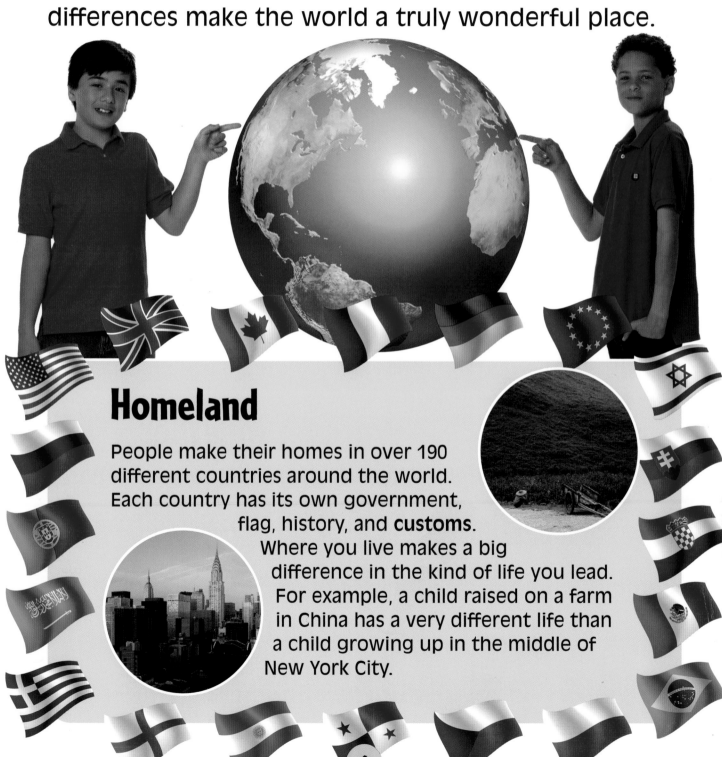

Homeland

People make their homes in over 190 different countries around the world. Each country has its own government, flag, history, and **customs**. Where you live makes a big difference in the kind of life you lead. For example, a child raised on a farm in China has a very different life than a child growing up in the middle of New York City.

A Lot of Languages

Many countries also have their own official language. Some countries have even more than one language. Here is a fact that you may find amazing! If you wanted to **communicate** with everybody in every country of the world, you'd need to speak over 6,500 different languages.

Rich and Poor

Some countries are wealthier than others. People living in poorer countries can have a hard time just feeding their families and providing homes. Children in poor countries sometimes can't go to school for as long as children in richer nations can. These children may need to leave school before they finish high school or even elementary school. They must go to work to earn money to help support their families.

Think About It

Are you proud of the country you live in? Do you think people who are born in another country are proud to live there? Do people have a right to hate your country just because it's different than theirs? Do you have a right to hate other people's countries just because they are different than yours?

COUNTRY CUSTOMS

Many countries or groups of countries have different customs. Customs are the common or usual ways people do things in their countries. You can find examples of different customs everywhere.

In Thailand, it is a custom to leave your shoes outside the door when you enter a home. If you walked inside a friend's house with your shoes on, you would insult him.

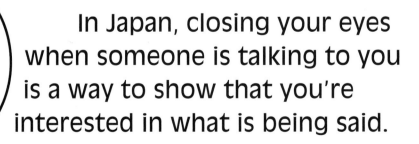

In Malaysia, people have a custom of pointing to something using their thumb instead of their index finger.

In France, when people make the OK sign, it means "zero."

In Japan, closing your eyes when someone is talking to you is a way to show that you're interested in what is being said.

Here at Home

In North America, people have different customs:

- They enter a house with their shoes on.
- They point with their index fingers.
- They use the OK sign to mean "all right."
- They keep their eyes open while listening to somebody talk.

 **Think About It**

You may think another country's customs are weird, but think carefully about it. Is it really any weirder to take your shoes off instead of leaving them on when you enter a house? Is closing your eyes when someone is talking really worse than keeping them open? Doesn't it all depend on what customs you are used to?

REGARDING RELIGION

People follow many different religions as well. Religions try to explain why we exist and how we should lead our lives. Some religions are built around faith in a single God. Some religions are built around a faith in a number of gods or goddesses. Some religions don't believe in God, gods, or goddesses at all.

Sometimes groups within the same religion have different beliefs. For example:

✝ Catholics and Protestants are both Christian. Catholics are guided by a religious leader called the Pope, but Protestants don't follow the Pope's teachings.

Pope Benedict XVI

☪ Shiites and Sunnis are both Muslim (Islamic), but they have different religious leaders and they go to different mosques.

Ayatollah Ali Khameini

More Than a Million

You might not have heard of all the religions on the following list. Each religion listed has more than a million followers.

The list is in alphabetical order.

African Traditional

Baha'i

Buddhism

Cao Dai

Christianity

Confucianism

Hinduism

Islam

Jainism

Juche

Judaism

Shinto

Sikhism

Spiritism

Tenrikyo

Taoism

Zoroastrianism

 Think About It

You may not agree with other people's religious beliefs. It is important, however, to respect their rights to hold those beliefs. How would you feel if someone made fun of your religion? Do you think it's okay to make fun of someone else's beliefs?

SKIN COLOR

Let's explore the reason people have different-colored skin. Point your elbow toward the ceiling. Look at the patch of skin on the inside of your upper arm. Scientists call this patch of skin your basic skin color because it almost never gets any sunlight. Basic skin color can range from dark black to pale white, with countless shades in between.

Color varies because people have different amounts of melanin in their skin. Melanin is a chemical that protects your body. It acts like a shield to block dangerous rays from the Sun called ultraviolet rays. Too many ultraviolet rays can cause skin diseases.

Light and Dark

Countries near Earth's **equator** have a lot of strong sunlight. People who come from those countries tend to have dark skin because they have more melanin. Countries far away from the equator get less sunlight. The sunlight is also weaker. People coming from those countries have light skin because they have less melanin.

EQUATOR

Think About It

Your basic skin color is probably not the color your **ancestors** had a few thousand years ago. As early humans moved around the planet, their skin color changed. When they lived in the tropics (closer to the equator), their skin got darker. As they moved away from the equator, their skin got lighter. Suppose a few of your ancestors could be brought to the present in a **time machine**. Suppose they had a different skin color than yours? How would you feel about their skin color and yours?

FAMILY STRUCTURE

Another reason people are different is because of their families. For example, kids may have

- no **siblings**;
- one or more siblings;
- a mother and a father;

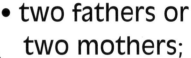

- one parent;
- two fathers or two mothers;
- **adoptive** or **foster parents**;
- grandparents, uncles, aunts, and cousins all living together.

Family structure affects the way people think, feel, and act. For example, an only child might feel comfortable spending a lot of time alone. On the other hand, a child from a large family might feel more comfortable having people around all the time.

Older or Younger

Birth order also makes a difference in how people feel and act. For example, the oldest child in a family is usually different than a middle child or the youngest. The oldest children may have to care for younger brothers and sisters. This added responsibility can make the oldest child a little more serious than the youngest.

Family Rules

Every family has different family and household rules. One family might make a lot of noise and reach for food instead of waiting for it to be passed. Other families might have rules, such as

- everyone does chores;
- no reading is allowed during meal times;
- kids have to make their beds every day;
- kids are not allowed to watch certain movies;
- kids can only play certain video games;
- kids don't spend time at home alone;
- kids have a strict bedtime;
- kids must do their homework as soon as they come home from school.

 **Think About It**

Think about how your beliefs have been influenced by others in your family. For example, if parents respect and value differences, their children will probably learn to respect and value differences as well.

PHYSICAL DIFFERENCES

Every single person in the world looks different. Even identical twins are not exactly the same. Besides skin color, physical differences include the following:

- height
- weight
- hair color and type (curly, straight, or wavy)
- eye color

Abilities and Talents

People also have different natural abilities and talents. For example, different people may have

- better athletic ability than others;
- more musical or artistic talent than others;
- an easier time learning languages or understanding math than others;
- a better ability to concentrate than others;
- an easier time making friends than others;
- a better imagination than others.

Disabilities and Special Needs

Some people need extra help to get certain everyday things done. They have special needs. For example, some kids might

- be **physically disabled** and need a wheelchair to move from place to place;
- have illnesses such as **asthma** that require special medicines;
- be blind or need special glasses to see;
- be deaf or hard of hearing and need help in communicating with others;
- be **mentally challenged** and have a harder time learning certain subjects.

 **Think About It**

This may sound like a silly question, but I want you to take it seriously. If you woke up tomorrow morning missing your little toe, would you be any less of a person? Suppose you woke up missing a foot or even a leg. Would you be any less of a valuable person? Suppose you woke up blind or deaf? Does your value as a human being depend upon how your body looks or works? Does it depend instead on who you are inside?

LIKES AND DISLIKES

People also differ about what they like and dislike:

- Some people like to ride roller coasters. Some people don't like scary rides at all.

- Some people love to play soccer. Some people would rather play chess.

- Some people like to be noisy. Some people like peace and quiet.

- Some people like to dress up. Some people like to wear jeans and a T-shirt.

- Some people love dogs and don't like cats. Some people love cats and don't care for dogs.

Ho, Hum, How Dull...

If everyone in the world was exactly the same, imagine how boring life would be. Everyone would speak the same way and have the same thoughts and feelings. Everyone would act the same way. No one would have any fresh ideas. There would never be any surprises. We would never learn anything new! Thank goodness, we have our differences.

Think About It

All the differences we've discussed so far affect a person's perception of the world. Perception has to do with the way the brain works with information it receives from the senses. Two people can look at the very same thing. Their perceptions about what they are seeing, however, can be very different. Your perceptions affect what you think and feel and how you act.

If this sounds confusing, read on for an explanation.

HALF EMPTY, HALF FULL

Look at the picture for a moment, and answer the question below.

Do you think this glass is half empty or half full? You might think it's half full, and your best friend might think it's half empty. Both answers are correct, and one answer is as good as another! Your answer will depend on what your brain does with the information it receives from your eyes. That is a good example of what perception means.

Your answer might even change from day to day. For example, if you're feeling unhappy, you might think the glass looks half empty. On the other hand, if you're feeling proud and happy, you might think the glass is half full.

Which Is Longer?

Here is another example of perception. Look at these two lines, and decide which horizontal line is the longest.

For most people, the top line looks longer than the bottom one. But believe it or not, these two lines are exactly the same length! It is only our perception that causes us to make a mistake.

Think About It

Your perception is just your perception. It may or may not be accurate. It is important to understand that this fact is true for everybody. When two people see the very same event, they can easily disagree about how or why it happened.

TUG OF WAR

Human beings have been fighting one another for thousands of years. The history of ancient Rome, Greece, Egypt, England, and China is filled with tales of wars lost and won. Right now, as you read this sentence, wars are being fought in dozens of places

around the world. Yet, if you asked people to choose between making war and living in peace, almost all would choose peace.

The Key is Cooperation

The key to living together is respecting our differences and learning how to cooperate. Countries need to cooperate. Different religions need to cooperate. Kids need to cooperate, too. When kids cooperate, they build happier neighborhoods and friendlier schools.

Pulling Together

Cooperation means working *with* others and not *against* them. Cooperation means building relationships and not destroying them. Cooperation means pulling together for a common cause. When people cooperate, they combine their different strengths and talents. Cooperation brings out the best in people.

Competition and Cooperation

Cooperation does not mean an end to competition. Without competition, we wouldn't have sports. Sports competition, however, is built on respect and not hatred. Athletes do their best to win, but they don't want to destroy their opponents. Athletes agree to play by rules. Creating those rules involves cooperation. Sportsmanship is another word for peaceful competition that is based upon cooperation.

Think About It

In ancient Greece, warring cities agreed to a short period of peace every four years. This peaceful time allowed their athletes to compete in the Olympic Games. Why do you think the Greeks did this? How could this competition build respect and increase understanding?

IT'S NATURAL

As we've learned, it is natural for everyone to see the world differently. Sometimes differences lead to arguments and **conflicts**. Conflicts can happen when people have different wishes and needs. Dealing with these differences can be very challenging. Luckily there are some skills you can learn to help you find ways to end the conflicts.

Remember Perception (Skill One)

Remind yourself that your way of seeing a **situation** is not the only way. Just because other people have different perceptions doesn't make them wrong. You may not understand exactly how they are seeing things, but you should at least understand why they might see things differently.

Decide What's Important
(Skill Two)

If you're involved in a conflict, you must make an important choice. What course of action will you take? Ask yourself the following question:

Which is more important—proving I'm right or finding out where we all agree?

Nobody can answer this question for you. You may feel that proving you're right is most important to you. If so, you will probably take a tough stand that could lead to an argument or fight. Or you may feel that finding common ground, or things you all agree on, is more important to you. If so, you will try to talk about the situation in a calm and open way.

SETTING GROUND RULES

(Skill Three)

When you're both ready to talk about the conflict, agree on some ground rules. Decide how you are going to treat each other. You might agree that

- you will take turns and speak one at a time;

- when someone is speaking, the other person will not **interrupt**;

- you will listen to the other person with respect;

- you will try to understand the other person's perception of the problem;

- you are going to attack the problem, not the person (That means no name-calling!);

- you will spend enough time to discuss the situation in detail.

To help make things fair, you could decide on a time limit for each person to speak. Also, be sure to agree on a place where you can talk freely.

Listen and Learn
(Skill Four)

Get ready to listen. Now is your chance to learn more about the conflict. Ask the other person to explain her or his perceptions of the situation. You might begin by saying something like, "I really want to understand how you see things. Is there something about the situation I don't understand? Will you please explain what has upset you?"

As the person speaks,

- face him directly and look him in the eyes;
- keep your temper and your other emotions under control;
- do not interrupt;
- make short listening statements, such as "uh huh," "yes,", and "I see," to show that you're paying attention;
- ask questions if there's something you don't understand when the other person is done speaking;
- **restate** what the person has said. Use your own words, so the other person knows you understood his thoughts and feelings;
- tell the other person you're grateful that he shared his perceptions.

MAKE YOUR CASE
(Skill Five)

Now it's your turn to talk about your perception of the problem. You can begin by saying something like, "I understand that what you said is true for you. It isn't true for me, though. Here is the way I feel."

When you speak,
- use a quiet, friendly tone of voice;
- don't blame;
- use "I" statements instead of "you" statements. For example, you might say, "This is the way I feel" instead of "You did something wrong."
- remind the other person of the ground rules if he or she interrupts you.

The Same Team
(Skill Six)

If you both feel you understand each other, take the next step. Start cooperating. Remind yourselves that you are now on the same team. You share the same goal— to find a solution that is as fair as possible to everyone involved.

Come up with as many solutions as possible. Don't worry if they seem silly or impossible at first. At this point, no ideas are right or wrong. Working together, you can come up with solutions that you both never thought of before. When you have a solution that both of you agree on,

- decide what each of you will do;
- take responsibility for doing what you say you will;
- give it your best shot.

Now You Know

We have been talking about dealing with differences, but I want you to remember something equally important. There is far more that unites us than divides us. If you look at our world from space, you won't see lines that divide our different countries. From space, our perceptions can change as we see a greater truth. For all our differences, we all belong to one family, and we all share one home. We belong to the family of life, and our home is the planet Earth.

GLOSSARY

adoptive parents Parents who raise a child to adulthood that they did not give birth to

ancestors People from whom an individual or group is descended

asthma A lung disease that causes breathing problems

birth order The order in which children are born in a family

communicate To give information, thoughts, or feelings to other people

conflicts Strong disagreements or fights

customs The typical ways of behaving or doing something

equator An imaginary line around the middle of Earth; the areas right next to the equator are warm and tropical

family structure The way a family is organized with the number of parents, caretakers, children, and/or other relatives

foster parents People who, for a time, live with and take care of a child whose parents can't take care of him or her

interrupt To stop a person from speaking

mentally challenged Describes people for whom it is more difficult to learn and remember

physically disabled Describes people who have difficulties with movement or their senses

restate To say something again using different words to express the same idea

siblings Brothers or sisters

situation The way things are; conditions

time machine A make-believe invention that moves a person through time and space; there are no actual time machines

FOR MORE INFORMATION

BOOKS

Accept and Value Each Person (Learning to Get Along).
Cheri J. Meiners, M.Ed. Free Spirit Publishing.

A Day in the Life of Children Around the World: A Collection of Short Stories. Kathy Kirk. Universe.

It's Our World, Too!: Young People Who Are Making a Difference: How They Do It—How You Can, Too! Phillip Hoose. Farrar, Straus and Giroux (BYR).

Let's Get Along!: Kids Talk About Tolerance.
Pamela Hill Nettleton, Amy Bailey Muehlenhardt. Picture Window Books.

WEB SITES

Planet Tolerance
www.tolerance.org/pt/index.html
This is a cool site where you can read stories about different cultures, draw a picture for a world mural, or make your very own storybook.

Child and Youth Health
www.cyh.com/HealthTopics/HealthTopicDetailsKids.aspx?
p=335&np=287&id=1521
This site has a lot of good information on how to find solutions to conflicts. You can read what kids have to say and take an online quiz to increase your understanding.

Peace Corps
www.peacecorps.gov/kids/
This is a terrific site where you can play a Peace Corps Kids Challenge interactive game to help villagers in another country lead healthier lives.

CDC Department of Human Services
www.cdc.gov/ncbddd/kids/kmalpage.htm
Go on an interactive kids' quest to learn more about disabilities and health.

Slim Goodbody
www.slimgoodbody.com
Discover loads of fun and free downloads for kids, teachers, and parents.

INDEX

About the Author
John Burstein (also known as Slim Goodbody) has been entertaining and educating children for over thirty years. His programs have been broadcast on CBS, PBS, Nickelodeon, USA, and Discovery. He has won numerous awards including the Parent's Choice Award and the President's Council's Fitness Leader Award. Currently, Mr. Burstein tours the country with his multimedia live show "Bodyology." For more information, please visit **slimgoodbody.com**.

Printed in the USA—CG